A Better Society We Should Create

Viable options and solutions to create a better Society

By

Emil Cosman

CONTENTS

Introduction

I can't remain indifferent to evil, injustice, misery, crass imperfection and inefficiency. Who could? I can tell you who could, the coward, the cloyed, the weak, the fool, the one who profits from and promotes those attributes, one without "character." The list is longer but I am sure you got the idea.

Due to my own convictions and my dislike of the system created for me by the ones having those up mentioned characteristics, I decided to write about what I have gathered in my soul like an unbearable pain in an attempt to make a difference.

I started from the principle that humans improve in order to make a better life for themselves, to evolve, to create, to reach and expand their intellectual, physical and spiritual limits offered/given by the extraordinary chance they were given by being born as humans.

I consider that a person's lack of desire of self improvement translates in a lost chance, it is like a being is endowed with reason, but that being refuses to use it. Should it not have been better to have given the quality of reason to another being that will use this quality in creating extraordinary things by using this "tool?" It is as if a person is endowed with fantastic physical qualities but that person decides not to use them, and instead sits down all day and wastes his physical qualities he is endowed with.

We, humans, are endowed with intellectual and physical qualities that we should not waste in our course of life but use these qualities to their maximum potential. Then, I considered that we need to have a certain mindset in order to employ our qualities, tools, and reach our limits of abilities. I tried to define this method, mindset, of analysis we need in order to define the "correct" attitude needed to efficiently succeed in the realm of reality. I used the principles of justice, personal responsibility, reciprocity, in analyzing, criticizing and finding the necessary solutions needed to create a more just, efficient, better society. I limited my analysis to just a few areas of our society, and since the details are numerous, I provided only a macro analysis of the existing problems in those areas.

The goal of this book is to incite the reader to see a different, superior alternative to our current society, an alternative closer to our limits of self-improvement in the middle of the current environment.

The goal of this book is not to make the reader feel good, or keep the reader entertained. The goal of this book is to provoke a reaction out of the reader, which will ultimately trigger action. This book has no hidden agenda; it states ideas in a naked shape, without sugarcoating or using political correctness in an attempt to make the reader feel comfortable. The goal is to point out what our fake, unnatural society leaves aside, hidden from the reader's comfort and sincere observation of facts.

The reader might feel insulted at times, might feel outraged with the ideas and suggestions comprised in this book, mainly because the reader might have been conditioned by our society and its masters, to think, see and reason in a certain way which promotes not the truth or objectivity, but the "feel good and inclusive attitude" of sheep-like masses.

If you are one of those individuals who easily get offended by other people's opinions or ideas, or if you are one of those people who do not want to offend anyone, therefore, never have a original opinion or idea which is in minority, then you should drop this book and return to your "feel good," out of reality life you are living.

Courage is needed for a reader in order to challenge his or her ideas, her core values learned or conditioned by others. Courage to acknowledge that you made mistakes or have been fooled for too long is needed in order for you to start over, with a new set of values and will, which will promote a healthy, true reality. The readers need courage to challenge their structures of thought.

This book is not the ultimate truth; it is a wake up call. The book will plainly state what many of us think that it should be done in order to create a better, healthy and meaningful society for people who know that self improvement stays at the foundation for developing a better person, therefore, a better society.

Emil Cosman

Chapter 1

Principles and Personal Improvement

Our own development, our own personal progress produces abilities. Abilities help the individual master the environment, and master his own self. Improving our personal qualities should result in an improvement of our personal lives. The improvement of our personal life means a higher standard of living, personal preoccupations of higher value, which are proportional with the intellectual development of the individual, and an easier and more luxurious life.

Through knowledge and reflection of our own actions and the environment we could better understand the phenomenon that rules life, and through knowledge and reflection we find the methods of self-improvement and progress.

The method people need to use in order to understand and create structures to help that process of reflection has a few clear steps.

The first requirement is people's direct exposure to the nature of the phenomenon they study, or better said, people need to directly experience the phenomenon.

Direct exposure/Direct experience

We must objectively observe the end result; the outcome of direct exposure to the phenomenon is a must. Objectivity is the minimum requirement in order to change something and to evolve.

Self-sincerity, or in other words, our personal sincerity with us, permits the observation of the result in a sincere and objective way, which should help attain the next step, which is the analysis.

Analyzing the results in an objective way and the inclusion of all data of the analysis should avoid personal preferences. The analysis must be non-preferential, therefore, objective.

The objective analysis, logical deduction of the phenomena that lead to the outcome one experiences, plus the understanding of the forces, connections and links which produced the phenomenon will permit one to master, control and change to phenomenon.

People need to memorize the mechanism that produced the phenomenon, and understand the actions that can change the phenomenon in order to produce different results.

Without personal will/desire to change, without desire/will to progress and without personal sincerity, that is avoiding a big ego, and without objectivity one cannot make a controlled change or a consistent personal progress.

Personal discipline and personal order in our actions lead to consistency and organized analysis.

Personal order and discipline lead to a systematic, controlled and cerebral advancement of one own self, or of any action a person will undertake.

A personal disappointment of a result in our progress is a healthy feeling, as long as it does not make us lose the idea, the direction of our goals of development. Self-dissatisfaction or dissatisfaction with our own work will instigate and intrigue us to start again in our own strive for personal or social progress; of any kind of progress where improvement is needed and benefic.

Efficiency must be very well calculated and the costs of personal improvement must be taken into consideration because by wasting energy and resources of any kind could prevent us or could slow us down from the process of improvement.

As individuals part of a society we must determine what actions, qualities and phenomena deserve to be improved and which ones, which are not needed for a person or for society should not. Priority of actions must be determined. I do not oppose people enjoying their little hobbies, but personal hobbies should not be placed ahead of personal improvement or before value. For example, in a society, the construction of a monument built out of cement must be avoided or postponed as long as the resources that would be used for the construction of the monument will use the resources needed for the constructions of a freeway, of a better freeway, or of the infrastructure in general. That does not mean that all the resources will be used only in building physical necessities and not used in creating things of an artistic value. What should be understood is that, for example, if an organism/human who is about to die of starvation has $50.00, the organism should not use the $50.00 for cigarettes, for a coat, for a painting or sculpture, but instead, the organism should use that $50.00 in order to stay alive in the first place, so the organism can grow, develop and create. Bad investment leads to the regression, or pure stagnation of the whole process.

Do absolute vales really exist? Do these absolute values exist without a human convention? Of course they exist. Qualities are used in the achievement or fulfillment of some goals that permit the individual to acquire or attain them. For example a raptor fish must use alongside camouflage, swift swimming speed in order to catch the prey. The speed offers the fish more chances to catch the prey. Very good eyesight is better and superior to weak eyesight. Animals, excepting man, are not capable of developing or improving their personal abilities in a conscious manner and in a structured manner. Humans can improve their qualities, abilities in a conscious and structured manner, in an efficient way, in a rational way. Doing things that run against the path to individual perfection is poor personal judgment and knowledge. We can improve our abilities.

A clear example which doesn't need a lot of philosophy, or a refined intellect to comprehend is comparing the work, success or development of the voice of a tenor with the voice of a singer of any other genre who's using the voice to create vocal sonority. I am not implying that classical music must be on everyone's liking or, for example everyone should like Luciano Pavarotti's voice. What I am saying is that everyone must understand and except that the voice, the vocal human capacity offered by Pavarotti is superior to any other human's on the planet. The wide number of octaves, the refinement, the musicality, the volume given by Pavarotti's voice is far superior for example to the voice of Justin Timberlake, Whitney Houston, Elvis Presley or any other singer. I am not talking about preferences in the musical or vocal genre. I am talking about a comparison between the development and progress of the vocal qualities of humans, vocal qualities in general, which we can understand and we agreed as humans as limits of human vocal abilities. Those limits could be extended or reached by personal training, setting aside genes. We could have various preferences but we must accept whose voice, whose vocal value is superior to whose. If people get upset about this, it only means that they are subjective, have an inferiority complex, or simply they're not sincere with themselves and will not be ever be capable of personal development or maybe only in a very limited way.

The value must be accepted and improved. People's personal inferiority complex or people's personal interest must be set aside if we want to achieve an efficient progress.

The human lack of strong will comes from a lack of understanding of the environment, of the person, and very importantly from the influence or from lack of influence of the environment on him. The lack of personal exposure to direct experience coming from the lack of need to understand the environment, a lack of personal conscious of life, or a lack of understanding of the environment leads to lack of a personal strong will.

An environment that will not challenge the individual, an environmental that offers a minimum requirement of action in order to survive, produces laziness, lack of desire to improve our personal abilities. Incentives are sometimes needed in order to make an individual act and improve in order to accede. But what are incentives that are acceptable, and which are the incentives that are not acceptable in producing a strong desire in an organism to improve?

Chapter 2

Assuming Personal Responsibility

By trying to shift responsibility for our own personal failures is not only lying to ourselves, but it is also blocking the access to information that could lead to the understanding of the causes that led to our failures or the effects which will lead inevitably to the omission of the focus, of the origin of the mistake which should be recognized, regardless of what or who it is, meaning us. Running away from responsibility stops us to correct our mistakes. This attitude opposes our own evolution, self-development, and will not prepare us for a success next time when we face the same circumstances. Running from responsibility is in part due to the feeling of fear from repercussions, shame, which in our mind will make our ego get smaller and tarnished. So that leads to our loss or diminished of our ascribed or achieved status in the society compared to other people. All this and the fact that is not just to avoid responsibility for your own actions, be it good or be it bad. Assuming responsibility for our personal actions doesn't mean that it should turn into a personal flagellation or social flagellation as long as the failure persists from various motives, as incapacity, laziness or from other personal defects which could be turned into qualities by using the same method explained before.

We sometimes must accept the fact that we have limited abilities, even in assuming responsibility, and even by trying to improve our personal qualities in order to avoid failure in the future we simply can't win because we reached our personal limitations. If that should be the case, we must accept the state of incapacity and we must avoid our exposure to those circumstances. This should be done only after we tried to improve our own abilities. We cannot run away from the face of challenge without even trying to oppose a fair effort to overcome it and start invoking inability, personal inability, or limitation. This is unacceptable.

By avoiding to assume our personal responsibility for our actions, our improvement is small or inexistent and most of all it is unjust. Even if we avoid accepting responsibility for our actions, in our soul and in our own egoistic world, we still remain with a feeling of injustice, which has a personal ramification.

By not changing or improving our personal value when facing some circumstances we will create a fear, personal fear every time when we would be facing those circumstances. What are we going to do then? Are we going to avoid, runaway, lie in order to avoid that situation? If so, who is going to be the one losing? It is going to be us, because by having weaknesses or a weak point, which we don't want to change in a quality, or in a satisfactory answer to that challenge will have us off balance. All we have to do is put a sincere and maximum effort in front of the challenge, otherwise we lose too much by running away from challenges and personal responsibility.

Chapter 3

Patience and Perseverance

It is well-known the proverb saying, "who's doing something hastily would not do a good job." That will not debated here and now. I will focus on the lack of patience in achieving qualities and achieving material goods during one's lifetime.

Failure should not inhibit a new attempt after a good preparation and reflection was given. Failure offers the chance of a reevaluation of personal abilities and resources. It offers the chance to analyze the unknown variables and known variable, or the observation of the phenomenon that influenced the results. Patience is necessary to observe changes in the phenomenon. Patience could not be achieved without perseverance.

Perseverance must be a determining factor in the desire to change, to grow, develop and improve. The effort for personal improvement must be perpetual, and without hollow spaces or depressions. The patience in achieving material objects, by postponing instant gratification, allows time to settle, to clearly analyze the depth of the situation, allowing us to make decisions after we accumulated sufficient information. A spoiled person or a moody person has a lot of work to do in achieving patience.

We should not make confusion between being spoiled or moody, and personality, individualism or with a free spirited individual. Being spoiled and being moody are states of haste and show incompatibility with self-control, one's inability to suppress one's personal impulses. This is something we mostly find in children. Young children have no self-discipline, or patience or lucidity to even assess the situation after a correct analysis or reflection. A hasty, spoiled or moody person will most likely make decisions in a hasty way without having enough information on the problem, or issue. Therefore, that person exposes himself to mistakes in a greater amount then if he would have given more time, analysis, observation and reflection. A person's decisions and options would be more variable after a longer time given to accumulate more information and data on the situation.

Chapter 4

Envy

Envy is the feeling that originates from a personal evaluation of self worth and then compared with the personal self worth of others. Envy feeds itself from other people's achievements compared with our personal lack of, or inferior achievements. Envy is a feeling of personal impotence projected onto a misguided direction, and the outcome is pain.

Other people's positive achievements should not make us minimize our personal achievements; on the contrary, it should promote the desire of self-improvement. Other people's achievements should be used as positive examples, which could probably show us the way to our own personal improvement. The feeling of pain, which results from envy, is negative as long as it does not promote or trigger action directed towards personal self-improvement, and instead it promotes actions meant to libel and denigrate other people's superior achievements. The feeling of pain resulting from envy is simply supported by personal inabilities based on a hurt ego, based on an inferiority complex directed towards other people's achievements. Moreover, it is even worse when the person who feels hurt believes that everybody else sees how incapable and unskilled he or she is.

The solution is simple. Other people's achievements, qualities, achievements should make us happy, because we can be used them as a guide, as an example that should result in a productive competition among the citizens of the society.

As I mentioned before, envy could be half forgiven or eliminated as long as it produces action for personal self-improvement, action to create positive competition among people.

Chapter 5

The Inferiority Complex

The inferiority complex is based on past frustrations, lack of achievements, or simply on an environment where the achievements of an individual are seen as being average, common, and not as a positive factor, which should be acknowledged and praised.

The lack of value and recognition, or the lack of acknowledgment of the special qualities and achievements produce an inferiority complex even in a person who has achievements, or positive and valuable personal qualities. An environment that does not acknowledge these positive and valuable achievements will frustrate the individual, and with time will produce a feeling of lack of personal self worth, of lack of value. Value must be recognized not as much as to generate an exaggerated ego, but it must be recognized as what it is: valuable achievements and personal qualities.

On the other hand, the lack of personal achievements or qualities must be recognized as what they are, and they could and maybe should generate an inferiority complex in a person who lacks personal qualities and achievements. If a person lacks value, then the inferiority complex is, and should be, rightfully present and dominate that particular individual's psyche. Only by personal achievements you have the right to attach value to your ego. If you did not have personal achievements or personal value, you should better start working towards achieving them.

In a society it is dangerous to create individuals with a false feeling of value only to give its members of the society a false impression of self-value in order to alleviate the pain of feeling the reality, that is the reality of lacking personal value. By disillusion, an inferior and without value individual, will live an illusion, and when this individual will be directly exposed to the environment, to reality, he would be ashamed to discover the system that turned him into a false individual. More importance must be given to reality than to the feelings of an individual. The solution is to help people acquire qualities and personal value through personal improvement, and not to create the illusion that they have them.

Self-esteem is a feeling generated by personal valuable actions and achievements, through personal development, and then compared with other individuals' qualities, value and achievements. A person who does not have personal value or achievements should not have self-esteem, because they don't and didn't create value. The false feeling of self-esteem, of self-worth is unjust and dangerous in a society that aims to justice, efficiency and self-improvement. It is just to have people with their feelings hurt if they do not have real valuable achievements and qualities.

I will use an example of some persons who have their feelings hurt by using the example of fat people. The fact that a person is overweight is a negative factor in itself. Obesity exposes a person to illness, physical limitation and death. Gaining weight in an unhealthy rate is negative. Setting aside the example of people who have real physiological deficiencies of thyroid for example, gaining weight is based on personal decisions and personal actions. It is our decision to eat a certain kind of food, a certain quantity of food and avoid physical effort. All these are examples of personal decisions. The lack of will or desire can't be claimed in order to defend a fat person. Lacks of will, desire or self-control are examples of personal defects of character. We should be ashamed if we have them, and we cannot invoke them and use them as valid arguments in order to justify our lack of personal responsibility.

Being fat has nothing to do with our personal achievements in a society, it is a physical defect, and it is an exposure to medical risks and generates an aesthetic appearance. There are people who despite the fact that they are overweight continue their struggle of personal self-improvement by recognizing that their physical condition is negative. Therefore, the overweight individuals who feel that they their feelings are hurt when their physical appearance is acknowledged must not try to force the rest of the society to avoid the obvious, or even dare to consider it as a negative condition. Those peoples who feel hurt by other people acknowledging their negative condition should better start changing their condition, instead of forcing the rest of the society to change their views. Those people must recognize that their condition is due to their personal actions and if they feel hurt, then the pain should make them act and change their condition. The solution is to improve your self-control, your desire to change and fight the urge to eat a lot and unhealthy, and engage in physical activities. We are the makers of our own destiny. Self-discipline is generated and improved through a lot of work, personal effort and through continuous action.

Chapter 6

Modesty, Excess and the Verbalization of Qualities

Why modesty? Why not verbalizing and showing off your personal value and let them be known? We all want truth to be the master, or do we want to avoid hurting anybody's feelings or anybody's ego, which nevertheless should exist only if one, has qualities? The inferiority complex and the hurt feelings idea should not precede truth.

Modesty is something that is imposed by the ones who feel inferior to other people of real value. If someone feels hurt or insulted by another person's real qualities shown to the public, than that person should better go and try to improve his or her own qualities and not impose the ones who really have good qualities to keep them for themselves to hide their pure, superior hard worked qualities or values, so the inferior, weak ones or without value can fell good. That attitude is a regressed attitude and must be avoided. We want to know and see what vale is, and what are the limits of humans in the society; values and qualities that must be reached and surpassed, not hidden and considered vain.

Personal qualities must be exposed, they must be showed off, but they do not have to be pushed into other people's eyes with the only goal of hurting, intimidating and injuring those others. If someone feels hurt by some other person's real quality exposed it is not the one person with qualities fault that he is in this kind of situation because even if that person would avoid showing his qualities, that would not change the condition of the week one who doesn't have that quality. Only a direct action of personal improvement, or personal perfection will make the one who feels weak or hurt get out of that state, and not by imposing others to hide their real values. A person who feels hurt by seeing other people's qualities by self improvement will never feel hurt again because he will have qualities as well, and he should also understand that these qualities differ from person-to-person, so a competition between individuals should appear and should be beneficial in helping everyone improve themselves by showing off your qualities. That self-improvement will also improve the society, so lack of modesty would not be a defect and modesty would not be a virtue. If we would all hide our qualities we would never improve ourselves, we would not have examples to follow or things to surpass or goals to reach. On the other hand whoever exposes his qualities in front of other people only to brag, that person loses the big picture, that is to improve your self for your own good, not to make everybody else gets sick of watching you.

Truth is always preferable to the feel good condition if a better society and world is to be created. We should see the truth and accept the truth because only by seeing it we can change, instead of trying to feel good and avoid seeing the truth if the truth shows us that we are not so good. If truth hurts someone, it's a healthy feeling as long as it triggers the action for perfection, for self-improvement. On the other hand if it triggers only a feeling of being hurt without personal action over improving your personal qualities then that person has a wrong way of thinking, a way of thinking that doesn't generate progress. For example, if one person is fat and someone tells that person that he or she is fat and that person does not do anything to change that condition but only cries and tries to make everybody else pretend that they do not observe that they are fat, and avoid any allusion or conversation about anything that has to do with fatness as a subject only so they do not feel hurt, it is wrong and counterproductive for the fat ones, and also it is unjust. If you are really uncomfortable with your condition, then change it! Do not impose others to accept it as a natural state, or to ignore it as if it doesn't exist. The problem is yours not anybody else's who observes it. You should not make everybody else avoid the subject by being afraid of making you feel uncomfortable which you should, and you should instead, gather the energy necessary to start changing your condition.

The argument sometimes used like "I always did it this way and I would not change anything," is an argument born out of fear, laziness and ego. Just because you've used a wrong method for such a long time it does not make that method being good or positive. It is absurd to continue making a mistake over and over again, or being inefficient only because other people did the same and it is has been done like this for long time, so inevitably "it must be" the best method. People are frightened to be found wrong but that that feeling opposes the idea of will, of necessity of changing into a better individual. We all make mistakes. If someone doesn't make a mistake, it means that that person is either dead, or that that person doesn't act, doesn't experience new things…to say the least.

Chapter 7
Individualism/Selfishness,
Social Spirit/Altruism

The answer to how someone should or what would be the benefic path for a person to reach personal improvement it's not clear-cut like black and white. The circumstances play a major role in the proportion of individualism versus the social spirit. We must first determine what the natural flow is, the better direction, and what is subordinated to what.

One direction starts from the society and goes towards the individual. Another direction starts from the individual and goes towards the society. We must accept that these two directions are not fixed and unchangeable, eternal and inviolable. Even if the first option seems to be the dominant option for the world, the second option is applied along side with the first option in fulfillment of the goals in small increments and might result in the fulfillment of the first option. The same scenario is true if the second option, which is the dominant one. The increments of the first option will be found alongside with the second option. The context dictates the option. The context depends on the values, goals, and well-established principles between the relationships between individuals who facilitate personal progress. Personal progress is intertwined with that social progress, and the personal progress dictates greatly the social progress. The social progress is the result of a personal progress due to competition and due to direct actions of personal perfection, of individual perfection. Social ideas of improvement come always from individuals who see them and then expose them to the society in order to help others in their striving for perfection. Ideas come from individuals who observe, understand and create in the framework of a phenomenon, and then produce methods by which personal progress becomes possible. The society is formed out of individuals and the individuals are not formed out of the society. Society is a derivate of the individual in contact with one another. The society is subordinate to the individual, to his personal interests, and the personal interests always appears to precede the social interest. Social interest has the role to help the individual's path to self-perfection in the context of more individuals gathered in a group. Personal progress is individual and will help the society because it will play the role of an example for other individuals in their own strive to perfection, so from one initial selfishness eventually towards a social altruism. Individualistic people will play the role of examples to the other members of the society by their personal achievements. The weaker individuals may copy or get inspired by the other individuals' achievements. People must have their own interest served and that will help the society by serving as amp, or sometimes as a negative example, which must be avoided if progress and personal improvement is the goal. That is determined by the ultimate goals of the achievements.

Chapter 8
Helping

Offering help should be done only when it helps improve ones' personal abilities and be avoided if it is only offered for material gains or finite positions. Help is given to someone to help that someone overcome an obstacle, to perfect himself otherwise the help offered is a wasted help. The same thing is true with the social help. Social help should be seen as helping the masses help themselves, to achieve personal power in order to overcome an obstacle. Offering funds, services that are non-reimbursable is a notion that leads to waste, and people receiving this kind of help would not understand anything, but will only take advantage of the resources given at the other person's expenses. This must be avoided.

For instance, if a person loses his job, he will not receive financial help without doing something in return. That person needs to produce something in return in order to receive financial help, something that will in time repay that service that was given in need. There is enough work to be done, work could be found everywhere, the only problem is the "preferential factor." People do not want to pick up jobs if they can just receive benefits for not doing anything. In a moral, ethical society staying home and receiving funds will not be an option. Everyone will be free to starve. Thee will be no law against self-starvation due to laziness or lack of desire to fight/work. The work that is offered in case people lose their jobs it's not something that people will choose from, people will accept the offer or not, the responsibility is theirs. There will be no laws forcing some members of the society to support other members of the society.

The taxes collected from the citizens will not be wasted; they will always need to return back into the funds pool they were taken from. It must be remembered that I am talking about a temporary help that will be paid back by the one who used it. The ones who use this kind of funds as well as the ones who manage these funds, help, must be supervised and controlled of how these funds are distributed and how the funds will be recollected from the ones who used them.

What are the legal punishments for breaking the law? We all make mistakes, but persevering in a mistake is monstrosity. If you keep on making mistakes and don't try to change those ways that lead to making mistakes could be seen as a ill will, indifference or incapacity. Each of these three situations must be solved in three different ways. All three of them will be structured and will have the goal to resolve some common problems. These problems are the reeducation, repayment of the damage, and of self-support in the penitentiary system.

Reeducation. By having someone incarcerated the society does not only try to keep that individual outside of the society where he committed harm. By incarcerating someone, the system will offer the incarcerated person new qualities by working in the system of the penitentiary, so when the time comes to be freed, that individual will have the necessary qualities and tools to use for personal success and for his success in the society.

Working while incarcerated will help repay the damages caused by breaking the law. When I say work it's not going to be a hard work, or killing work, or something that would make the person destroy or degrade him. That will be discussed later. The person who was incarcerated not only has to pay for his own reeducation, pay back the damages produces by his actions, but also that person needs to pay the costs associated with living in prison. The society should not have to support a person who broke the law and his incarcerated, so that person could just sit and watch TV, or sleep and build his muscles while incarcerated. There could be a situation when the incarcerated person will refuse to participate in the reeducation program, or refuse to help repay the damage, or pay for his expenses while in prison. One thing could be said for sure: a person will not be kept alive using other citizens' funds from the society. If someone doesn't want to participate in the program, and will not try to improve his abilities, neither try to repay the damages and will not try to improve himself in order to be a positive member of the society when getting out of jail, such a person's attitude does not coincide with the need and the will of self perfection which will probably lead in the future to new law breaking actions, hurt individuals and stolen goods. Such an individual will not have many options to choose from, in other words, his options will be either, or.

Chapter 9

The Penitentiary System

The goal of the penitentiary system is that of helping people improve and develop new abilities which will be used in the society after being liberated. It also has the aim to help people reimburse the damaged property due to their actions.

The system will offer a work schedule of up to 10 hours per day with one day off. It will provide the rest of the day with an educational program and free time. The program will offer hot showers, meals and a bed to sleep. All the amities that the incarcerated person will use will be paid through that person's work. The work will be viewed as a normal job, the only things that would make a difference would be that the person would be supervised and the work efficiency will be high.

In case of rebellions inactivity or refusal to participate, that will lead to a recalculation of the payment that the person needs to pay, together with a new reevaluation of his social reeducation. The period of detention will add to the time and education of the person. There will be no corporal punishment but in extreme cases the firing squad could solve a problem where a person refuses to participate and lost his desire to survive. After all, this system is not a high school, but a benevolent prison.

Any abuse from any side of the system will be punished. The patience of the system would not be unlimited, the elimination of the individuals would be possible as a rule in extreme situations as: attempts to escape, a definite refusal to participate in the program, violence directed towards others who participate or against the personnel of the program. The penitentiaries will not be buildings having iron bars and concrete walls with diffuse lights and narrow spaces. It will be more like a camp with barracks and surrounded with prevention fences, guarded by armed guards with guns and ammunition ready to be used. The so-called mutinies or attempts to break out of prison in-group will be dealt with by means of using ammunition.

Chapter 10

Justice and its Distribution,

Preferential Group Status and Death Penalty

The distribution of justice will always be done through argumentation, through facts and ideas, through the means of free debate. A free debate means the liberty of any person to support his thesis by bringing evidences, supported by facts, regardless of the popularity, or lack of popularity of the facts or evidence brought up to support the thesis.

There will be no taboos in the realm of ideas. There will be no interdictions of using certain ideas, instead, any idea will be used, regardless of how harsh it is or might sound.

Political correctness will be avoided or nonexistent. Any idea, anything could be debated, including the Earth's shape, the irrelevance of the divinity, or the irrelevance of any preferential status of a group, which will not exist anyway.

There will be no ridicule of an idea without bringing contra arguments, because ridicule is the proof of narrow intellect and low character. The "fight" will be an intellectual fight. It will be a battle of ideas and knowledge and will be based on the quantity and quality of the ideas, resources, facts and proofs. The winner will not be decided by ridicule or irony. Who degrades himself to such "little" games of inferior value will identify himself with the person who already lost the debate already. Then, these kinds of persons must be revealed for their narrow mind, and of course help them to improve their knowledge.

Lack of will to learn limits a person's knowledge; therefore, the recognition of a low intellectual status, of an inferior person and not of one with intellectual qualities will be a normal state. This kind of persons must be avoided, or helped, or placed in such works equivalent to their potential, to their intellectual potential that is. These persons must be recognized as such, which is: intellectual stagnates. These kind of individuals could not be elected as leaders of people or ideas, unless they privately produce their own financial stability, but on the realm of the intellect and value, they must be recognizable for what they are, again, intellectual stagnates.

If a person proves to know more than other people on a subject, the superior status of that person on the matter must be recognized. That is regardless of the status of that person in the society overall. Anyone has the right to challenge that person to a battle of ideas and arguments, and the status of that person in the society will not prove that he holds the ultimate truth or should be listened more than other person who has more knowledge than status. The battlefield is the battlefield of ideas, the one who knows more and reasons better, who uses logic and so on, will be the person who will be "right" and who will win the battle.

By direct challenge, the intellectual dominance of an individual will be determined, not by diplomas or certificates. It is true that certificates and diplomas help, but they do not dictate obedience. For example, let's talk about a factory worker who is well read versus a PhD graduate. The factory worker's words and knowledge will have the same weight as the individual who has a PhD. A person demonstrates quality and value of intellect, by engaging in direct battle of ideas and arguments. The factory worker should not be silenced, or not taken seriously only because he is "just a worker." It is possible that the factory worker could know more about the subject of the discussion than the other person who is educated. The winner is determined by knowledge, not by credentials.

Group preferential status. This notion will be nonexistent in the society. The personal value will be the determining factor of a person's worth, not his or her group affiliation. Discrimination will be done based on personal value. There will be no preferential status, or reparations of any kind about the so called past discrimination for any ancestors by other group's ancestors. We will all start as equals; the only thing that will differentiate us will be the personal quality of each of us. You either have it or you don't. If you have it you will be high up in the society, if you don't have it, you will be down below. Nobody will be promoted on the basis of group affiliation in a preferential way. If this will happen, then the punishment is a major one.

Death penalty. If a man kills another man I do not see why death penalty should not be a valid and fair option. The relatives of the victim's closest of kin would take the decision for death penalty or a life time term. In the case we have more than one victim one single choice or vote in favor of capital punishment should veto all the other victims relatives' votes. Convictions for major infractions could be of a certain length of time, but major infractions could also be punished with capital punishment in case of pedophilia, rape and forced sodomy.

Chapter 11

Homosexuality, Supernatural Believes,

God, Marriage, Adultery, Incest and Polygamy

Homosexuality is the penetration by a male sexual organ of the anus of another male. The "so-called" feminine homosexuality is nothing but a sexual game of sexual exaltation between two or more women. Sexual normality is defined by the sexual act through which reproduction, giving birth is followed. Sex is not something like the so-called "oral sex," or "anal sex" or who knows what kind of other games of sexual exultation. Sex equals masculine sexual organ penetrating the feminine sexual organ. Whoever wants to bring counterarguments or disagrees with this clear definition only has to take a look at nature and see that this is the general, overwhelming rule; and if there is an anomaly, than that is a perversion of the general rule.

Homosexuality will not be illegal. It will only be occurring in some people's bedrooms and nothing more. The same thing is the case off bestiality. Bestiality will not be illegal but it must not get out in the open, outside of one's house or the privacy of the pervert's life. In case one is observed, seen performing bestiality, he will not be prosecuted as long as that person could prove that he tried to stay hidden and that his goal was not to advertise it or be seen by others with intent.

God. Anyone has the freedom to believe in any kind of strange idea as long as it is not forcefully imposed to others, and also it's not used as a valid argument in an intellectual, logical and factual debate. Anyone has the right to debate ideas of supernatural without being afraid of being prosecuted or afraid of any repercussions. God will not be taken or used as a face value argument. God will be taken as an idea that brings comfort to certain people who otherwise could not live their daily lives. Invoking the divinity in a debate or conversation as proof or argument would decrease or nullify the debate's intellectual value. Divinity will be something only personal and nothing more. Anyone has the right to believe that a duck is God if they want, and there is where the use and existence of the divinity ends.

Marriage, adultery and incest. Marriage is a personal choice not a social necessity. Anyone can get married and marriage has no sanctity or holy value. It is only a contract between two individuals of opposed sex that could be terminated at any moment. Concubinage has no negative connotation; it is based on each person's liberty to decide of not getting married or getting in a contract with one another. It has the same value in a society and has no stigma associated with it.

It is not illegal to commit adultery and the matter should concern only the married couple, it is not anybody else's business what's happening in other person's personal life. This situation must or must not be solved, and if it is to be solved it is to be solved only by the two signatories of the marriage certificate.

Polygamy. The society should not be against polygamy but some regulations of the functions of the polygamy system must be put in place. Polygyny also has the same value as Polygamy. Certain laws concerning the offspring coming out of these types of relationships will be needed. The number of the children resulting out of these systems will be based on the ability of the parents to care financially for their children.

Incest. I am not against sexual acts performed between two blood related grownups even if they are of the 1st° of skin. That is their business; their decision, and it must not be qualified as something positive in the society, but rather neutral. The problem starts when children are born out of these close related unions. The society will not support such situation and will not support the children. The individuals involved must assume the responsibility for their actions. Charity organizations can help if they want under one condition: they have to insure permanency, they must guarantee that they will take care of those persons and will not drop them along the way, so it's not going to be something temporary. The handicapped people who can support themselves are okay in a society unless they start being a burden for the society. The society, the elements that form the society must evolve and perfect themselves. This is the rule that should guide the society. Accepting regressive elements or offering an environment for these elements to procreate and thrive is against the notion of perfectionism, evolution and improvement. We could not allow to become a society where the number of the handicaps will grow in such a manner that the genetic pool will be infected by their genetic irregularities, because in the end it will destroy humanity, will eliminate it.

Chapter 12

The Right to Die

Any person has the right and freedom to commit suicide or ask another person to help him commit suicide. Euthanasia is the right of anyone to choose. The person who accepts to help other persons to commit suicide would not be punished and will not be socially stigmatized. That would be a normal state of life as it is for a person who goes to a restaurant. A declaration of support would be signed and maybe one witness, legal or not legal, would be needed, and that's it, and you are ready to go. After all we are the makers of our destinies.

It is not the State's role to make sure its citizens decide to live or die on their own accord. The State's role is to make sure the laws of the Land, the freedoms and liberties of its citizens are respected. Why should a law prohibiting suicide exist? What is the purpose of such a law? It is simply absurd to try to prevent people from wanting to die if they do not want to live any longer. It is also ridiculous to criminalize the act of suicide. Even to punish a fail attempt to commit suicide. Ultimately it is our life and we are the owners of ourselves, therefore the sole masters of our own lives.

Chapter 13

Abortion

It is the right of any woman to stop the pregnancy up to three months after conception, after three months of pregnancy, abortion becomes a legal problem. The biological father has the right to veto the mother's decision to have an abortion on the condition that he will be the only legal parent when the child will be born. Under such circumstances, the mother will be legally declared "dead." The father will assume 100% responsibility in raising the child if the mother chooses to commit an abortion but the father vetoed it. The mother will have no right of any kind to the newborn.

If the future mother wants to keep the baby, but the future father does not want the baby, then the same rule applies, he is legally declared "dead," but must financially support the costs associated with pregnancy, if any.

Chapter 14

Adoption

Adoption would be perfectly legal but it would be regulated in such a way that it will follow the racial lines of the nation. It would be based on the racial choice because we want to avoid the "shock" and personal stress the child will experience when the child will realize that he is black leaving in a Asian or white family for example. Avoiding the child's stress or personal discomfort together with the genetic differences will play the major role in adoptions. It could be like having a dog being raised by a family of cats and vice versa. Adoption will not be a business; rather it will be a benevolent care for another human being. The costs associated with the adopting process will be minor, but the responsibility will be high for the parents who decide to adopt.

Chapter 15

The Educational System

The educational system will be divided in three spheres of accessibility, the public education, offered by the state, the private education, offered by independent education institutions, and family or personal education, offered by the family.

The main areas/categories of study will be: real science, social science, arts and physical education. The population has to mandatory graduate middle school. The standards will be set by the state in the real science, and in some social science. Physical education will be mandatory. Martial arts will be mandatory because a person needs to learn the spirit of "direct" competition through his or hers own abilities and not helped by surrounding environment or other people. Martial arts also develop self-discipline, self-control and self-confidence, and that happens when under stress. Courage will not be developed in a sterile environment, free from pain, risks and stress.

Anyone will be free to pursue his or her academic education over the eighth grade, like high school or university. The requirements and acquirements of credentials by professors will be very high and it would be based on competition and hard examinations/tests. We can't afford having professors who could be challenged and embarrassed by their own students' knowledge and moreover, on their own field of education. Professional schools will be public and private. The accreditation of these institutions will be done by examinations. Anyone can choose to be homeschooled by the family and not go and attend any class in a private or public institution, but to get accredited and be granted a diploma some state examinations must be passed.

Social sciences will have standards and examination and will be based initially on fixed, real, hard facts, which will not be open for interpretations. The education in social

science, as history, will be offered in a platonic manner. The liberty of expression in arts will be flexible, but the accent will be placed on value and perfection. Value and perfection will be standards by which the arts will be created and spread. The arts dealing with a philosophical depth will be used to promote a healthy self-improvement, develop ideas, and promote physical, intellectual and moral improvement. The promotion of degenerate arts of human degeneracy or social degeneracy will be forbidden.

Chapter 16

Drugs and Alcohol

The State will have the monopoly on alcohol. Any person over 18 years of age could drink alcohol legally. There will be no limit in the quantity of alcohol consumption for a person. Anyone can get drunk and pass out. The problem is if someone under the influence gets in trouble with the law while intoxicated. The punishments will be drastically.

The State will have the monopoly on drugs. I am not referring only to prescription medications; I am referring to mood altering drugs as Heroin, Cocaine, Marijuana, Methamphetamines and so on.

One must be 20 years of age in order to use them, and can use as many drugs as he or she would want. The problem arises only when legal infractions occur while under the influence of drugs. The punishment will be incarceration and reeducation. There is only one answer from the State to those involved in the "black" market for alcohol and drugs: elimination of the individuals involved, of the links, and confiscation of the properties of those implicated. There will not be such a notion as the "transfer" of funds/property from those implicated in illegal trafficking to other relatives. If those funds were achieved by illegally selling drugs and alcohol, then the entire wealth will be confiscated, including banking accounts. There will be no juridical loopholes to save someone who will try to avoid having his or her funds confiscated, or shelter their properties to his relatives if the funds were acquired through illegal sale or production of drugs and alcohol. There would be no protection of any kind for state employees, regardless of their position/status in state employment. The law will be the same for everyone and applied to all.

Chapter 17

Lawyers and Judges

A system must be designed in such a way in order to try to find what actually happened and not to try to help someone avoid being discovered as being guilty. The search for the facts, the search for the truth will be the goal of the lawyers and of the judges. If a decision will be taken erroneous by a judge, it will be easily reversed and changed if truth would be found to be otherwise. What matters is to find out the truth in whatever happened, and not to defend the so-called "honor" of a judge. The honor is achieved by doing honorable acts; dishonor abides by the same rules. The punishments for corruptions will be harsh, regardless of the gravity of the act of corruption.

An overregulated society is a less free society. Assuming personal responsibility will be one of the main pillars of which the society will be built. How pathetic and fake are those signs attached to some professional trucks by some companies saying: "safety is my goal," when we all know the business' goal is to make a profit, as it is the driver's goal too.

The sickening "safety" movement will be replaced with having personal ability and have personal responsibility. The ridiculous high number of pitiful lawsuits will be drastically reduced and the need of an army of lawyers and judges will be reduced to an effective number of well-educated and able people.

Chapter 18

The Banking System

There will be no private banks. The role of the banks will be to finance businesses, entrepreneurs and projects. Interest rates will be minimal, acceptable and accessible. The National Bank will work in the interest of the society, promoting the fulfillment of the ideal of personal development.

The balance of power between people, business at one side and the banks will be reversed, and will take its natural course, with the former regaining its main status in the balance. The current balance of power and importance between the up mentioned sides in our society is an unnatural, unhealthy and unjust. The producers are at the whelm of an institution that would not exist without the producers, how stupid that is? A bank would not exist without workers and their businesses, and even though, the banks in our current society dictate and are I the driver's seat when actually the banks should be there to assist and help, not to oversee and dictated the businesses and workers.

Chapter 19

The Army

There will be a mandatory military training time for men, and voluntary military training time for women. The requirements will be the same for both sexes. The military training will be designed as it is in Switzerland. Every person who fulfilled the military training will own military automatic weapons and military ammunition. The right to bear arms will not be infringed for those without mental handicaps or criminal convictions, like felonies. The right to bare arms in plain view or concealed will be granted, and the requirements will be loose as long as there are no mental diagnosis or criminal convictions. In case of misuse of military weaponry, the criminal convictions will be harsh. There will be active military personnel, as career commanders and maintenance personnel.

The focus will be placed on the high tech armament and not on the number or tanks and rifles. Rapid intervention forces, or Special Forces will be the backbone of the military. Their training will be hrs and they will be the highest trained military professionals.

Chapter 20

The Police Force

The police officers will be armed and will have that right and freedom to use their weapons when circumstances allow. The right to use their weapons would not be infringed as long as the police officer's safety is endangered.

The unauthorized and violent mass demonstrations that degenerate could be stopped with police or military firepower. Mass demonstrations are free and will be authorized as long as they are peaceful.

The freedom of travel abroad will not be infringed and will be free. The freedom of immigration will be granted, but the immigration will be strictly planned and structured. The immigration requirements will be strict and that will be based on intellectual, racial, cultural, ethnic and ability criteria. The accepted immigrants will have to sign certain documents stating their loyalty to the country. Citizenship will be granted after certain tests of language, geography, history, and ideology and after at least 15 years of being physically present inside the country, of course after a green card was granted first.

Chapter 21

Scientific Research, Cloning

The goal of science is to discover, explain and produce. Scientific research will put more focus on research than on ethics. That does not mean that hurting someone is allowed in the name of science. But if that someone is willing to get hurt in the name of science, then that takes precedent to the so call code of ethics in science. If the goal surpasses the sacrifice, usually when includes animals used for scientific research, the importance of the goal will be greater than the lives of some animals. If a scientific experiment requires lets say 100 cats to be used in order to find a cure for cancer, than it will be done. It is happening even in the current society, when terminally ill people accept to be used as guinea pigs by some pharmaceutical companies in testing their drugs that possibly work on the patients. Those drugs have side effects of course.

Human cloning will be legal. The only debate will be on what will be the role and status of the cloned humans in the society. The debate should be about their equality with the other members of the society and about avoiding exploitation of the cloned humans. It goes without saying that cloning anything else will be legal. Probably cloning will be a state monopoly so no private institution can abuse the cloned humans.

Chapter 22

The Mess Media

There will be only state owned mess media. The mass media will promote the social and personal interest of the individuals on their path to perfection. If private mass media would be allowed to exist it will be scrutinized by certain state agencies. The private mass media will be easily closed in cases of abuse or if they use their outlets for foreign interests or agents, or against the ideology of self-personal improvement. The movie and entertainment industry will promote a healthy view of the society, with ideals of personal development. The books will be used in the same manner as the movies and entertainment industry. Educating the society is the goal, and the mass media will be one of the tools used in achieving that goal.

The society must be informed, the society must be educated, and the society must be entertained. The national interest will never be sacrificed or tarnished by the media. Yes, there will be contradictions and conflicting interpretations of certain events, but the national interest will be paramount.

The Insurance System

People will not be forced to ensure their houses or cars. But in case of inability of paying damages that occurred after an accident, the payment will be reimbursed through work during the incarceration.

Chapter 23

Mass Democracy

The democratic system of decision-making in a society should be used as long as it produces an efficient improvement and it is based on the principle of justice. Ideas always come from one individual and not from a group. When a group comes up with an idea the idea certainly came from an individual first, or an individual build an idea on other individual's ideas. Decision-making implies courage, knowledge and responsibility. It is difficult to punish a mass of people who made a decision in case the outcome is negative, moreover, if the decision was made based on a majority of votes taken within the group. The easiest and one of the most outrageous examples is the Parliament. If a Parliament makes an erroneous decision in the name of the country, the system's way to punish the members, the people who voted for the mistake, will be by voting them out in a few years from now. This is wrong. It is true that people make mistakes, but it is just only when people assume their responsibility for their mistakes and try to change them into successful acts. I once heard someone arguing that if the members of the Parliament would be immediately punished if they made a wrong decision, then nobody would want to make decisions anymore, or even be part of a government or a Parliament. The counter argument is that by this immediate punishment the cowards will be excluded from leadership positions, positions that actually need courage by definition. Cowards should not lead. Cowards, for the advantage of cowards, bring the argument I just presented to you. A while ago I heard the argument that if in a society a government or a parliament could be changed whenever its members make a mistake, then everything will be stagnant and nobody will dare to make a decision. That could be true, but at least we will have good decisions. Mistakes have different levels of gravity, and the process of changing a group could be difficult, but well thought methods and efficient methods to change them could be designed and applied. These details could be discussed in another chapter.

Therefore, it is better to have decisions coming from one individual because in case of a mistake the individual could be changed quicker than a group. Also, the individual will certainly know that he assumes his responsibility for the decisions he makes and he can't hide behind other people, or other people's votes. And evade responsibility due to a number. But who will be the referees or the people who would analyze the gravity of a mistake? A group, yes, another group, but an authoritarian group. There will not be an institution that will have its members appointed or voted in office for life, as it is the case in the US Supreme Court. Crass mistakes will lead to swift demotions and penalties.

Universal right to vote? Yes and no. It is a mistake to endow any biped with a full vote, regardless of the biped's level of intelligence, knowledge or value. That is because an individual who lacks knowledge and value will be able to nullify the vote of another individual who is well informed, knowledgeable and with value, because that is not only unjust, but it is also inefficient.

I propose the introduction of aptitude tests in order to determine the vote value for each individual. The tests will be of political science, history, geography, macro and micro. A person should be able to vote only when that person understands the problem we face as a country, as a society. A system will be designed where tests of certain complexity will allow people to have a quarter of a vote, a half of a vote, three quarters of a vote, and a full vote.

Paying taxes will also play a role in the value of the vote a person will have. A frequent use of referendum will be utilized for important decisions for the country.

Mass democracy in an uneducated, uncultured society, or in a society that is educated by the "so-called" Free Press is just a masquerade. In a society where its members go and vote thinking that they are informed because they are repeatedly told that they are educated, but actually the Free Press is the opinion maker can't be a positive situation.

Something must be done to change the low level of educational requirements in the Universities. The university graduates really think that they are qualified and they are really intellectuals. Why, because they acquired a diploma, so that should make them pass as intellectuals. No. Knowledge, not diplomas acquired from institutions that call themselves educational institutions that actually are run like businesses will play a role in what we are as individuals, and of course in the level and quality of our votes.

I had the chance to meet a lot of university graduates who consider themselves as being intellectuals and very well inform members of the society just because they graduated college. Most of these individual were proud that they are informed by the mass media with whatever the mass media offered them. They also believe that they are capable of understanding where the propaganda spread by mass media starts and where it ends, or that they are able to avoid the subliminal messages they are bombarded with, or elude being conditioned by the mass media. The ability to understand and set aside propaganda, the puppeteers behind the curtains, and the forces that maneuver the information from the shadows in a sick society is what matters, not a diploma, or parroting the information given and carefully provided for consumption by some people who actually dictate what you are allowed to be informed about, and what you are not allowed to be informed about. The real critical spirit is based first on analyzing a problem from as many angles as possible, regardless if they are favorable or not favorable to our ideas. We want Truth to be Paramount, we want Truth to dominate the feelings, we want Reason to dominate the feelings and so decisions will be made in a responsible and knowledgeable way. The false feeling of believing that you are informed and capable of making decisions based only on one piece of information from one source, or from more sources but which are all owned by the same owners, and controlled by the same puppeteers, is dangerous, and has no intellectual value. The diversity of the sources must correspond with the diversity of those who make a profit from spreading the information.

In conclusion, the ideas come from the head of one person not out of a group's head. Not every citizen will have the right to vote only because he is a citizen. The ones who will have the right to vote will have limited or full voting power. That decision of the value of the vote will be based on strict tests, which must be passed and determine the value of the vote of all individuals. Personal responsibility will be at the foundation of changing the decision makers.

Chapter 24

The Qualities of a Leader

A leader by definition is the person who commands a group. The best scenario is when a group has as its leader its best individual, with the best skills need to lead the group in the best direction so the group will benefit from the decisions made by the most skilled individual in the group. Let's say a group elects its leader base on charisma. Then the group will not have as a leader the best individual endowed with the best skills to lead the group in the right direction based on knowledge and so on, but will have a charismatic individual who might not have neither the intelligence, nor the knowledge needed to lead the group in the best direction, so the group will be stuck with a charismatic, incapable leader. That is why a leader must prove that he has certain qualities that allow him to lead in a responsible and efficient way, and his election or ascendance in the leadership position must be based on the proven skills he has. If the group is dumb, then the leader will either elect a dumb leader, or the pool from which the leader will rise will be of low intelligence and quality. The leader's qualities, or lack of qualities show the quality or lack of quality of the members of the society. It is true that other forces may influence the election and ascendance of leaders, like corruption or mass media influence. In the so-called democratic systems where their leaders are elected by vote, the elected leaders form their cabinet with "capable," "skilled" ministers, advisers and cabinet members. These appointed individuals will present their decisions or opinions to the elected official, lets say the President, who will need to trust them since he has not gotten a clue about the certain branch of the government. Therefore, the President is at the whelm of the appointed officials who lead state departments. These state officials might have their own interests, connections and maybe allegiances that do not coincide with the President's or the country's. The leader must be able to have a certain level of knowledge and understanding in order to be able to actively participate in the cabinet's meetings and make decisions in a informed and responsible manner, otherwise, those cabinet members or chiefs of the state departments can do whatever they want since the President is "dumb." The qualities of a leader are: knowledge, intelligence, courage, strong willed, macro and micro vision, realism, moderation, patience, power of persuasion, physical Health and mental health, and direct life experience.

Chapter 25

The Role of the Religion in the Society

Every religion could be practiced without fear of state interference. Religion will not influence the state's decisions. Religion will not be taught in public or state schools. Religion is a personal, intimate issue and will not be used to justify decisions or mass demonstrations that aim to make the masses act in a political or social direction. Religious discrimination and discrimination coming from religion will be illegal. The state will not fund or give any preferential treatment to any religious denomination or religious institutions, which will be financially supported through their own donations and private sponsors. Religion will be something that will not be seen in the social and intra-human sphere. Religion will help those elements in the society, who need stability, moral support, and those who cannot satisfy those necessities on their own.

The religious dogmas or religious writings will not be used as valid arguments in public debates, outside of their religious debates. The idea that the country's unity comes from the nation first will be thought. Region will not be allowed to play a dismembering role in society and that is because of the philosophical factor that will dictate the group unity that will be based on nation. Notions of people, citizens, nationality that belongs to one single unity would be the force that will keep the individuals and the society united. There will be no state religion. The religious leaders will be recognized only in their religious organizations and not in the public organizations where they will be recognized as citizens of the nation.

Chapter 26

The Economic System

The economic system will be a capitalist economic system. The system will have the citizen at its center, then the profit. The system will not be a wild capitalist system; it will have limits. The capital will be invested abroad only if the profits, or part of the profits will return in the country as investments. Personal profit will be limited; part of the companies' profits will be reinvested in the companies in order to grow, become more productive and be more competitive.

The owners will have sufficient profit for themselves in order to be rich. How well a person works will be the measure of each person's standard of living. There will be no unemployment, or it will be only for a short period of time. There will be some state companies that will do the vital job for the country. These state owned companies will be mainly overseeing the country's infrastructure or the military potential, but there will be private companies that will compete among one another for projects in the vital spheres of the country.

The inventors and their patents will be heftily paid and recognized. Citizens who will bring honor to the country through their outstanding value will be generously paid and honored.

A system based on points will determine the minimum wage for the working people. The so-called minimum wage will take effect only if the worker will demonstrate the needed value to ask for the minimum wage. In other words, if your efficiency and skills are low than you will not qualify for minimum wage. You can ask for governmental services, in order to improve your work worth, in order to become profitable. You will pay for these services…eventually. There will be no social programs designed to use the producer's taxes in order to support individuals who refuse to work or avoid working. The social programs will be designed to temporarily help people in need to improve their skills in order to be competitive on the job market and the services they used will be paid back.

Chapter 27

The Health Care System

The health care system will function on the same principle of personal responsibility and reimbursement. Every person who is employed, and that is almost everybody, will benefit from medical care. The temporarily unemployed will also benefit from medical care, but they will repay the costs of medical care if used, as soon as they will get a job. One of the requirements must be that they actively look for employment and if unsuccessful, the government agency in charge of helping the unemployed will make sure that they will have a job. There is always work to be done. There are always jobs available to get people employed. The only "inconvenient" aspect that intervenes between employment and unemployment is the desire to work, sometimes regardless of the nature of the work found and offered. There will be a zero tolerance for those unemployed who try to use health care when unemployed and refuse to accept jobs offered by governmental agencies after they failed to find employment on their own. There will not be such a situation when an unemployed stays home, pretends to look for employment, and "milk" the health care system. I assure you that such a person will find a job, or a job will be found for him, and will repay the health care costs cumulated during his unemployment period. If charities are willing to financially support such individuals, the government will not interfere.

It is inadmissible to be forced to pay about 1,000.00 Dollars for a root canal and another 1,000.00 Dollars for a crown if uninsured in the current state of affairs in our present society. It is outrageous to file for bankruptcy after having a costly surgery and be employed, but without benefits. That misfortune of undergoing a surgery should not ruin a person's life and family, moreover if that person has a job. Just imagine the costs associated for a child who need surgery. If his parents do not have medical insurance through their employer, the family is in danger of losing the battle with life. The argument that people may have private insurance is unacceptable due to the unreasonable costs associated with acquiring such a private insurance.

The bottom line is: if a person is employed, that person and his family should have health care benefits.

Chapter 28

Costs for Education, Daycare, and Maternity

Public education will be free. Rigorous tests will need to be passed in order to accede to high school, stay in high school and hard admission tests will need to be passed for university admissions. Some schoolbooks will be provided at no costs, and some will need to be acquired by buying them. Attending a university must be based on intelligence, and not on the amount of money the applicants have.

Public kindergartens and day care centers will be free. Private ones can charge as much money they would like. The number of public kindergartens and day care centers will be allocated based on census data.

There will be paid prenatal leave and maternity leave opportunity for mothers or fathers who want to take the role of primary caretakers. That is of course in case the mother is employed during her pregnancy. The maternity leave compensation will be about 80% of the salary earned during employment. The maternity period will be up to two years.

Chapter 29

The Society, Minimum Standards (Last Thoughts)

The natural and basic rule of life is: organisms must work to acquire their means of survival, food. Organisms must do something productive that will allow them to physically survive. The better an organism adapts to an environment, the better chances to survive and thrive will have. Adaptation, which is improvement of skills, comes only if an organism is directly exposed to the environment's challenges. A sheltered, easier environment will produce a slow or no improvement of an organism.

The alternative we have if we do not do anything.

We will have a Society where some citizens are forcefully made to pay for other citizens' services, which will benefit neither the first group of citizens, nor the society in the long run. This is simply unjust.

We will have a Society where free and open debate will not exist due to taboo subjects or restricted ideas that will limit the volume and depth of knowledge. Political correctness correlated with the taboo subjects will limit the Truth; therefore will cripple the scientific advancements by avoiding "offensive" truths to be exposed in order to sustain the improvement process.

We will have a Society that will offer a sheltered and an unnatural environment, hence producing a self satisfied, slow, lazy and unhealthy individual.

We will have a society where value and quality are replaced with un unnatural dogma that supports the idea of equality in abilities, an unjust promotion of individuals based on the idea that avoiding hurting people's feelings is more important than being just, being of value and having real abilities.

We will have a Society where will promote a less competitive environment because we do not want to lower anybody's self esteem, and because we are thought that we should achieve the same results under the same environment since we are all "equal" in our abilities.

We will have a Society where "big donors" will control the electoral democratic system, the mass media and the political class. We will have an electorate that will be manipulated by a controlled mass media. We will have leaders with "charisma" that will be the sufficient requirement in order to be elected, which will lower the real qualities and competencies of a must-be leader.

We will have a Society where its citizens will really believe that Universities, which provide a diploma at monetary cost, and a very low standard in admissions and its curriculum, educate them. This society will create the illusion of an intellectual class.

We will have a society that financially supports criminals in prison, by forcing its law-abiding citizens to pay for this support without receiving anything in return. This is simply unjust.

We will have a society that teaches us that personal responsibility could be shifted, quality ignored, that "second chances" are available at an infinite number, that we are all "winners" without personal effort and value, that "feeling good" and avoiding offending others are more important than Truth, and being "safe" is to be preferred to courage, risk taking and a strong personality.

If you believe that all these are good in a society, then do nothing to change it, just look around you and you will notice these current realities. If you believe in truth, justice, personal responsibility, self-improvement, value, courage, unity and hard work, then start doing something to change the unnatural society we currently live in. I will be by your side! Together will succeed in creating a better society!